MAKING
THE
RIGHT
CHOICE

MAKING THE RIGHT CHOICE
No More Stress with the IRS
Copyright © 2022 Jon Neal

Expert
Press
www.ExpertPress.net

ISBN: 978-1-956220-25-4

Expert Press
2 Shepard Hills Court
Little Rock, AR 72223
www.ExpertPress.net

Editing by Dana De Greff
Copyediting by Wendy Lukasiewicz
Proofreading by Lori Price
Text design and composition by Emily Fritz
Cover design by Casey Fritz

MAKING THE RIGHT CHOICE

No More Stress with the IRS

Jon Neal, CPA, MST, CPFP, CTM

Contents

Introduction

This may come as a surprise, but when I was in high school, I didn't have dreams of becoming a certified public accountant (CPA). I wanted to become a music teacher. I've always loved music, and I've always loved helping people, so it felt right to me at the time. And while the music part didn't work out, as a CPA, I still get to do what I love: help people learn new things. I also know from firsthand experience that any involvement with the Internal Revenue Service (IRS) can be stressful, anxiety-producing, or worse—it can, without exaggeration, ruin your life.

Part of my motivation to write this book is to educate people so they can better understand the ins and outs of taxes. But the other part is to help people avoid making poor choices, because I once made some ghastly choices that got me into a lot of trouble with the IRS. If what I learned from my experiences can stop you from doing the same, then my work here is done.

Many people have this almost deathly fear of the IRS. I get it, but it doesn't have to be that way. You don't have to live in fear of getting a dreaded notice from the government, lose sleep wondering if you filed your taxes correctly, or forgo filing altogether (which, by the way, is definitely not a good idea). Ideally, you'll read this book and realize that there are right ways to do things when it comes to filing taxes, as well as smarter ways to do things. You can avoid getting in trouble, and rest assured that if you are in trouble, I'll help you find a way out.

Here's the thing: If you already have problems with the IRS and need help resolving them, this book will do just that. If you don't have problems but want to better understand taxes and your finances and avoid making mistakes, this book will do that too. If you're curious to become more knowledgeable about a topic that vexes so many, you've also come to the right place. Whether you're an individual or a business owner, the chapters I've included here are meant to get your life back, and, ideally, make it more lucrative.

So let's start where it all begins—with you.

Chapter 1
Why Individuals Need to File Taxes

To say that individuals need to file taxes may seem like the most obvious of statements, but the truth is that millions of people every year fail to file their taxes. If you think about how humans operate, though, it shouldn't come as a huge surprise. We're often driven by fear, which can cause action or inaction, and in the case of filing taxes, believe me when I say that the IRS will figure you out eventually. I've had clients come to me who didn't file for one year, and others who didn't file for decades. It's quite common, but it's never too late to get on the right path. In this chapter, we'll get into the importance of filing your taxes, but we'll also discuss how to file them correctly, what common mistakes people make and how to avoid them, and what solutions are available if you're in a bind. I'll also share some more insight on my story.

Here's the short answer as to why you need to file your taxes: By law, any person or married couple whose gross income is over a certain dollar amount, or who earned more than $400 from self-employment, must file a federal income tax return. Simple enough, right? In theory, yes, but you might be surprised how many of my clients don't realize they've been filing their taxes incorrectly. There are a lot of rules and exceptions on what is exempt from taxes. To know exactly what is excluded by law, you can look at Internal Revenue Code Section 61, which provides details on what isn't taxable, such as Veterans Affairs disability benefits, certain other types of disability pay, and life insurance, for the most part. On the other hand, if you pick up a twenty-dollar bill off the street, you're legally bound to report that as income because found money isn't exempt.

Filing taxes is the law. Taxes are revenue that fuel the US federal government and pay for things like Medicare and Medicaid, education, land management, parks, public health services, and more. Which is why if you don't pay, or don't pay the right amount, the IRS will figure it out sooner or later, and you'll risk owing penalties and interest, or, in the most extreme cases, you'll be sent to jail. You might think that the IRS is too busy or that a few thousand dollars won't be missed, but from personal experience, I can say that the gamble isn't worth it—not by a long shot.

There's something about the IRS that gets people worked up, scared, and anxious. For good reason. You see characters in the movies or on television, or occasionally read about real-life wealthy celebrities, who are fined or sent to jail for not paying taxes. The thing is, though, that all this fear surrounding the IRS—or anything, reall—is due to a lack of knowledge or understanding. A lot of people don't know what they can do to take advantage—legally—of the tax laws, let alone how to set up arrangements so that they don't have their bank accounts levied, their paychecks garnished, or their house or car taken away from them.

This is why CPAs and enrolled agents are so important. We're the people who know how to navigate the rules, regulations, and jargon, and we understand the issues you may have or the trouble you may already be in. I don't know how many times I've seen the weight lifted off my clients' shoulders when I've said, "Yes, I can help you, and here's what you have to do." The IRS isn't going to empty out your bank account, take your house, or throw you in jail. One of the most amazing things about what I do is that I can see the results with my clients. It may take a while, but I can resolve whatever burdensome situation you're dealing with.

I love what I do because I get to help people and make a real difference in their lives, and much of this comes from my upbringing. My mother was a teacher, as was my sister before she retired, and my dad always treated the people he worked with fairly and respectfully. Even when I was in high school, I was helping people. My first real job was at McDonald's. I did really well there because I often helped my coworkers understand what was going on and how to do things. As far as I can tell, I've always been that way, able to both help and relate to people, to meet them where they need to be met.

Lessons Learned the Hard Way

Another reason I feel like I'm uniquely qualified to help people with their IRS problems is that I, too, have had my problems with the IRS. And not small ones, either. It may sound strange, but most of the trouble I got into was because I was trying to help other people. Hindsight is always 20/20, of course, but I did rather foolish things trying to make other people, and myself, money. I ended up using the government's money for a long period of time to do that instead of paying payroll taxes. When I eventually got caught, the code section for willful failure to collect or pay over tax—29 USC 7202(a)—would forever be burned in my brain.

What code Section 7202 comes down to is that anyone who willfully fails to collect or truthfully account for and pay over withholding tax can be sent to prison for up to five years and fined up to $10,000. Serious stuff, in other words, and I can honestly say I didn't think I would get caught. I was planning to pay back the money, and it was kind of easy not to pay the government when nobody was standing over my shoulder. I kept telling myself that I'd get out of the hole I was in and fix it real soon.

It was in the middle of tax season in 2007. I had a client who ran a trucking company, and he needed money to pay some of his bills. He had another investor in the business, and I had money. The loan was supposed to be short-term, so I gave him some money as a temporary fix. The cash flow was supposed to be resolved pretty quickly, but then he paid me back a couple of months later with a bad check. At that point, the logical thing to do would have been to bow out and take the loss. The human side of me, the side that we know all too well and makes mistakes, decided that I had to cover my bills. Because I didn't have the money to do this, I made a foolish choice: I used the government as my bank.

I always paid my employees first, but then I used the tax money to pay my other bills and to fund other businesses, and it compounded and compounded, until one day, in 2013, two men with badges and guns—IRS criminal agents—showed up at my office. I remember that I was the only one there that day, and the men showed me their badges and asked if I knew that I had unpaid payroll taxes, which, of course, I knew. And that's when they started their investigation. In September 2016, I pled guilty to failure of withholding and depositing payroll taxes, section 7202, and was sentenced to five months in a federal prison camp and two years of extended supervision after that. I was also required to pay restitution of the taxes I hadn't paid before.

The funny thing is that nobody I worked with at The Neal Group was really shocked that this was going on, but they didn't know how bad it was because I hadn't divulged all the details. When I got caught, a couple of people jumped ship, which was understandable, but the rest of my employees stood by me. I was very lucky in that sense. In my personal life, my wife was furious with me, and my children were angry and disappointed, but they all stuck with me too. I consider myself a fortunate man to have been given a second chance. It could have been a lot worse, and I don't take that for granted. After I was found out, it was a huge relief, in a way. I could begin the work to correct my mistakes and move on, which is part of why I wrote this book. I want everyone out there to know that if you've made a mistake, it's never too late to make amends. Maybe from reading my story, you'll avoid some of the errors I made. I know from firsthand experience how scary it is to feel like the IRS is pursuing you and to know that you owe money, but believe me, it's always better to be honest.

After the IRS confronted me, the first thing I had to do was notify the State of Wisconsin that I had been convicted of a felony. The state did a perfunctory investigation and determined that my CPA license had to be revoked, and there were two routes I could take. I could voluntarily surrender my CPA license and never be a CPA again, or the state could revoke my license, and I could appeal to get it back in the future. I wasn't ready to abandon my career, so I took the second option. The good thing is that after a few years of probation, the state allowed me to regain my CPA license. I had to take the ethics exam again and pass it, and it goes without saying that I did, but it was worth the wait and time spent. The IRS, which regulates CPAs, also revoked my ability to represent clients before them, to prepare appeals, and anything else like that. That suspension usually goes for five years, but I got my ability to practice back in three.

.   The point of this story obviously isn't to show how clever I was or to scare anyone. I promise. The point is to show you that because I made a few stupid decisions, because I didn't think things through, and because I assumed nobody would notice what I was doing, I ended up having to pay a lot of money and losing a lot of time. The truth—the hardest thing to accept—is that everything I did, every error I committed, I didn't have to do. I could have asked my friends, or coworkers, or family, or heck, even a CPA for help. I do wish I had had people there to help me, to get me out of a hard place, to advise me not to lie to myself that everything would work out. I wish I had known that doing something wrong to help other people isn't worth it, and the smartest thing to do is to bite the bullet and ask for help. However, none of us can go back in time. All we can do is live in the present and plan as best we can for the future.

How to Best File Taxes

The first thing you need to do when filing your taxes is to become a sort of collector, one who is as meticulous as possible. If you're the super organized type who has been keeping good records and compiling documents all along, you won't have any trouble. But if you aren't that type, start gathering all the information you can: forms, documents, statements, anything that has to do with your income and expenses over the past year. With almost everything online these days, you should be able to easily access all your records.

Where it may get a bit trickier, of course, is if you don't have an official full-time employer and are a gig person, such as a musician, writer, or artist. In that case, then you really need to have your records together. You may be getting paid with cash or through digital payment networks like Venmo, PayPal, or Zelle, and you need to report all of it to the IRS. A common misconception people have is that paying under the table isn't really illegal. Don't fall into that trap! Once you've done all your collecting, depending on the complexity of your situation, you may want to have someone who knows what they're doing prepare your taxes for you. The price of hiring a CPA may seem like a big expense, but in the long run, a professional can prevent you from paying too much or too little. Hiring out is the best idea if you're not well versed in what I like to call "IRS-speak."

A good amount of complexity, jargon, and rules surround taxes and tax laws, which is why CPAs exist—to help you. For some people, filing their taxes every year is as simple as receiving a W-2 tax form that shows what you've earned from your employer, how much taxes have been withheld from your paycheck, the benefits provided to you, and other information, all in one document, which is nice and easy. But if you're a contract or freelance worker (a nonpayroll worker), then you'll probably have some 1099-NEC forms, and so gathering and summarizing your information can be a little more time-consuming. Your employers need to send these forms to you. If, for some reason, they haven't or you don't have them, make sure to get them as soon as possible by going back to the source of the income and requesting a copy.

Outside of employment income and expenses, you also have to take into account tax credits and deductions for individuals, which many people don't even know exist. The credits you claim can increase your refund or significantly lower the amount of taxes you owe, so it's important to know where and how to claim them. They can really make a huge difference in your life. The main credits that people claim, according to the IRS, are family and dependent credits, as well as homeowner, health care, education, income, and savings credits.

Deductions, on the other hand, can reduce the amount of your income before you calculate your taxes owed. Those deductions can be itemized: educational, investment, and work-and health care-related. This information can be found online; it's just a matter of sorting through the information to know what you can and cannot deduct.

Not claiming the proper credits and deductions mentioned, as well as not properly showing your income for the year, can be dangerous because most of this information is sent to the IRS anyway. When the IRS gets your information, they match that up with information from other sources, such as your employer. If there's something missing, you'll most likely get a notice from the IRS showing what you owe, plus interest and penalties. The IRS doesn't know about your deductions, though, so their calculation of tax due will be much higher. This is why it's up to you to report all your income and deductions in an accurate and timely manner—not only for your sanity but for your wallet.

These days, since the advent of electronic filing, it's pretty easy to file taxes. Your information goes from your computer straight to the IRS's computer. But again, if your situation is more complicated, or you don't know what you can claim or deduct, using a professional is a great idea and will save you money in the long run.

Common Mistakes People Make

Over the years as a CPA, I've seen just about every mistake an individual could make (sometimes unintentional, sometimes not) on their tax returns. I've seen married couples file as single people and each claims a child because they can get more money back that way. I've heard stories about tax preparers who make up dependents so that their clients can get more money back on their tax returns. More recently, I've seen a lot of people filing false W-2 forms— making up jobs and employers they don't have. People will also increase their wage amounts, say from $20,000 to $35,000 so that they get a $10,000 refund, or they'll claim deductions they aren't entitled to, such as declaring a rental property they don't have and taking deductions they aren't entitled to.

Now, when your tax return doesn't match the information the IRS has, that's when you have a problem, which is why you need to keep all your records straight. If you get a CP2000 notice, also known as an *underreporter inquiry,* that means that you probably owe taxes, and penalties, for missing income you didn't provide.

Another area where people often mess up or get confused is not taking the credits they're entitled to. For example, there's an energy credit for putting windows in your house, there's a credit for setting up a retirement plan when you're in business for yourself, and there's a foreign tax credit for owning foreign stocks. There are credits for dependents who are not children, and now there are credits for college and university tuition. You'd be surprised how many people don't take their credits or don't claim all the deductions they may be entitled to. The laws do change often, so you have to keep up with all that, which is where using an expert comes in handy.

What to Do If You've Made a Mistake

Assuming that the IRS hasn't already notified you, or the state, that you've made a mistake on your tax return, you need to file an amended tax return as soon as possible and report what was missing, whether it was income credit or a deduction. The amendment allows you to admit that you messed up on your taxes, and you will pay the IRS before they contact you (thereby avoiding any penalties). This is the best-case scenario and is not at all uncommon. If you're going to do this, what is known as a *post action review*, go online and get the forms to amend your tax return, or you can use a professional to help you fill it out and file it in a timely manner.

On the other hand—and this is important to note because a lot of people make this mistake—if the IRS sends you a notice before you know you've done anything wrong, and they state that you forgot to report something or that you owe a certain amount of money, don't blindly accept it as the gospel truth. I know that sounds strange, but a whopping 75 to 80 percent of IRS notices sent out to taxpayers are incorrect. Why? Because the IRS works off the information that they have, and maybe you reported it some other way, or you forgot to send in forms, or the totals simply added up wrong. A client came to me recently because the IRS said he owed $28,000, but it was actually $1,800. A huge difference, and for many, a life-changing difference.

If you have a reasonable explanation for your error, or errors, there's a good chance the IRS will waive any penalties. Yes, they will charge you interest, but it's possible that they will waive the penalties, known as *first-time abatement*, which basically tells the IRS that you've never had this issue before, you made an honest mistake, and you won't do it again. And if you meet certain requirements of not having that issue in the last three years, filing your returns in a timely manner, and paying your taxes, odds are you'll be forgiven. The IRS will also reduce or abate penalties through what is called *reasonable cause*. Situations that affected your mental and emotional state, such as suffering a natural disaster or dealing with a spouse who is deathly ill, would be considered reasonable causes to have errors or tardiness in reporting.

Despite what people think, the IRS can have a more human and understanding side when it comes to errors or late filing. A good instance to point to, for example, is when you've lost all your records or had trouble getting a copy of your W-2 because of a natural disaster. With Hurricane Katrina and the fires in Colorado, the IRS gave blanket extensions for people to file their return or pay taxes due. Things happen in life, and they understand that—to an extent. Just make sure you don't abuse it or make it a habit.

What to Do If You Get Audited

Being audited by the IRS means that something's not matching up in your records. You're either under some sort of investigation, or you've already been investigated and you owe a certain amount. This might sound silly to some, but the most important thing to do is *open the notice*. Seriously, I have people who come in with stacks of unopened letters from the IRS, wishfully thinking that not opening them will make the problem go away. Such avoidant behavior can cause unnecessary heartache.

The most common notice you'll get from the IRS is the CP2000, from the automated underreporting unit. It's a simple form, really. It states what you owe, plus a fee on whatever that amount is. That could be for under-payment or negligence penalty in interest. There are also other correspondence audits where you become kind of an independent contractor. In that case, you would file a Schedule C. You may also get an office audit, which the IRS doesn't use much anymore. You could also receive a field audit, where IRS agents come to your office and go through records, but that's typically for bigger businesses.

You don't have to turn your life upside down or panic if you get a notice from the IRS, but you do need to get your documents together. If you want to save money and reduce stress, enlisting the help of a professional isn't a bad idea. We understand IRS-speak and have dealt with many different types of cases and clients, much more than the average person. Again, reading all the IRS notices and doing your due diligence is super important. Don't take anything at face value, and make sure you ask your CPA as many questions as you need to get the full answer.

In the next chapter, we'll focus more on businesses. So if you have one, or you're thinking about starting one, you'll want to pay close attention.

Chapter 2

Why Businesses Need to File Taxes

Just because you exist as a business doesn't mean you don't have to file or pay taxes—if only it were that simple! That being said, there are a few different types of business taxes, and we'll go over them here so that you won't file your taxes incorrectly or get hit with any penalties. The type of business you run will determine what taxes you need to pay and how to pay them. The IRS outlines five general types of taxes: income tax, estimated taxes, self-employment tax, employment taxes, and excise tax.

☑ **Income Tax.** When it comes to income tax, if you have a business, then it's pretty simple. You need to file an annual income tax return, the same as someone filing as an individual. The form you use to do this, however, depends on how your business is set up and organized, which is why it's important that you closely follow the IRS guidelines when it comes to structure, or hire an expert to help you.

☑ **Estimated Taxes.** Estimated taxes are what you pay on income, even if you are self-employed. You need to pay these at regular intervals throughout the year, either online or by mail.

☑ **Self-employment Tax.** Self-employment tax, or SE tax, is for those who work for themselves, which still falls under being a business. These payments contribute to the coverage you get under Social Security, which you will most likely need at some point later in life, including retirement benefits, hospital insurance benefits, and disability benefits.

If you fall under this category, then you'll go on to a Schedule C and pay the SE tax and file a Schedule SE, with Form 1040. There are rules with these forms, too, and special exceptions are made for those in the notary public or state and local government employees, for instance. Refer to the IRS website under Self-Employment Tax for more details to make sure you don't get fined or penalized for filling something out incorrectly.

☑ **Employment Tax.** As a business, when you have employees working for you, you have more responsibilities. You need to pay them, of course, but you also need to file forms that include Social Security and Medicare taxes, federal income tax withholding, and federal unemployment tax. These must be paid, no matter what, and this is where I had my issues. Take a lesson from me: Don't withhold or underpay anything. It's just not worth it.

☑ **Excise Taxes.** This last option is for very specific areas of business, such as environmental taxes, heavy vehicles, retail sale of trailers, and wagering activities. Again, check out the particulars through the IRS website for all these options to make sure you're not missing anything and to avoid being penalized. It's a lot to check, but it's worth it to handle your business taxes the right way.

Not Everyone Is an S Corporation

Most small businesses want to be treated as S corporations, formerly known as *subchapter S corporations*. These are businesses that choose to pass corporate income, losses, deductions, and credits on to their shareholders, in turn making them report their income and losses on their personal tax returns. This lets S corporations avoid double taxation on their corporate income, and it gives them limited liability protections, meaning the assets are protected from possible claims from contracts or litigation, a very good thing to have as a business.

The caveat, however, is that while everyone wants to be an S corporation, not everyone is one. The IRS is now looking hard at those kinds of corporations to see if the owners are paying what's called *reasonable compensation*. Some owners are underpaying themselves, for example, because one of the features of an S corporation is that you can take out distributions or dividends and avoid paying payroll taxes.

Some people then think, *Well, if I don't have to pay payroll taxes on my distributions, I'll just take all my money out as distributions. I'm paying the same income tax but can avoid paying payroll taxes* (which are a little over 15 percent). There is a line on the form for S corporations called "compensation of officers," and if that line has a zero, that kind of raises red flags with the IRS. That's when they'll come in and say, "Your form shows that you took distributions of $200,000 but no salary, so we're going to reclassify that $200,000 as salary, and now you owe us payroll taxes and penalties for being too greedy."

I had this sort of situation recently with a client who was a landscaper. One year he took $300,000 out of the business and paid himself in dividends (not through payroll). And wouldn't you know it, the IRS rushed in and audited him. "This isn't reasonable," they told him. "We're going to reclassify that $300,000 as payroll and tax you for payroll. Now you owe us in taxes, penalties, and interest." When he hired me to help him, I did my research and uncovered some reports stating what a person with a high school degree and a career in landscaping with twenty years of experience usually makes. I learned that landscapers get paid an average of $60,000, yet my client made $90,000. He was getting paid 50 percent more than the industry standard. In the end, I was able to support that he was being paid a reasonable compensation for what he did, and the rest was coming from his employees.

Overall, there are certain things that businesses are more suspect on, and there are certain things that individuals are more suspect on, so you should be very careful not to make errors that draw attention. For businesses, the IRS watches out for owners trying to run personal expenses as business expenses. For example, you own a construction company and build your own house, but you then try to run all the materials, subcontractors, and other related costs through the business account as opposed to a personal one. A lot of this comes down to common sense, but the mistakes still happen over and over again.

The Difference between filing as an Individual versus as a Business

More important than understanding the differences between filing as an individual versus filing as a business is to understand that you must file taxes no matter if you're filing as an individual or a business. You should always keep good books and records as a baseline. Apart from that, if you're filing as a corporation, you should be observing more legal formalities, some of which I went into in this chapter. To understand all the nuances and to file correctly, make it a habit to check the IRS website, and if you can, make use of a professional so you don't incur any unnecessary fines or penalties.

Common Mistakes Businesses Make

As mentioned earlier, many businesses want to be categorized as an S corporation, and if you are one, then you must pay the owners and officers reasonable salaries for what they do. Big no-nos, yet quite common occurrences, are business owners running their personal expenses through the business, not reporting all their expenses, and thinking that payment in cash isn't income. The latter isn't as common as it was in the past because more people pay with credit cards or through apps.

A new development that is less uncertain these days concerns Bitcoin transactions and other sorts of e-commerce. The IRS is currently developing an audit program to go after entities like Coinbase that act as clearinghouses, to see who they have as customers and then go after those customers and records to see what has been done. I've already worked with clients in the cryptocurrency world and recently did a return for a client who had $1 million in gains in cryptocurrency. It seems there will be many new developments to come in the future.

Another common error businesses make is not having budgets or any sort of forecast for their financial future. They don't keep good records, so they don't have anything to support what's going on, and they kind of wing it when it comes to filing taxes. Winging it leads to taking risks, and that can often get companies into hot water. If your business doesn't keep good records, then start doing so right now. I promise you it will go a long way for your financial stability and peace of mind.

The biggest mistakes for businesses include using round numbers for expenses or income, guesstimating expenses or income, not reporting corporate employee salaries, having higher-than-necessary meal deductions, having higher-than-necessary home office deductions, reporting lower income, and claiming business losses for several years. However, take heed that, in general, more things can go wrong with an individual filer than with a business because the IRS tends to scrutinize individuals more.

The Errors I Made

When it comes to making mistakes, mine were pure and simple: I didn't pay the taxes I needed to pay. I withheld money from the IRS, and I used it for other purposes. In essence, I used the money to fund other businesses that were for a client or a business that I didn't have an ownership interest in but had a financial interest in. I kept thinking that very soon, right around the corner, I'd be able to pay everything back. But the reality was that I couldn't. What happened with me wasn't really a mistake. It was intentional. I was thinking a lot about who do I pay first: my supplier or the IRS? I chose my supplier, which was the wrong choice.

Solutions If You Made a Mistake as a Business

The good news is, just as with an individual, if you make a mistake as a business, you can always amend your tax return. For example, you can reclassify employees to pay payroll taxes instead of giving them 1099s, or you can get into a payment arrangement with the IRS or the state to pay the taxes you owe. Unlike the letters sent to individuals, usually when it comes to businesses, the amount you owe in those letters is correct. It's still a good idea to double check, just in case.

A last note on this: If you've been in trouble once, you'll be on the IRS's radar, and they'll always check back to see if you've cleaned up your act.

What to Do If You Get Audited

As with those who file as individuals, when your business is being audited by the IRS, that means that something's not matching up in the records. You may have to pay a tax penalty and interest, but fortunately, the good news is that it's not very common to be audited by the IRS as a business, especially the smaller ones. The bigger you are, and the more assets you own, particularly for sole proprietorships and C corporations, the greater chance you have of being audited. S corporations and LLCs tend to have lower audit rates, but either way, having good records and being honest will avoid any trouble.

The most common type of audit for businesses is a correspondence audit, where the IRS will let you know in writing of a possible mistake or mistakes in your return. Be sure to open those. Again, this is where good record keeping and documentation is key, and if you need extra help, there's no shame in hiring a professional.

Don't panic if you get a notice from the IRS. Get your documents together, and if you want to save money and stress, enlist the help of a professional. It's the smart thing to do. We understand IRS-speak and have dealt with many different types of cases and clients, much more than the average person. Again, reading all the notices and doing your due diligence are crucial. Don't take anything at face value, and ask as many questions as you need to get the answers you're looking for.

Chapter 3

What Happens When You Don't Pay Taxes

If you find yourself in the situation where you haven't paid your taxes, the first thing to recognize is that you're not alone—not by a long shot. Millions of people find themselves in the same situation every year, and there are ways to fix your mistakes (or at least clean them up). Assuming your return was filed correctly and the tax is due, several options are available, more than most people realize. Ignore the fear that if you mess up once or don't pay your taxes at all, the world will end. It won't. I know it doesn't from real-life experience. But it is true that you will need to get your affairs in order.

This chapter will help determine which path is right for you and therefore relieve any anxiety you may be having around taxes. It's one thing to make a mistake and try to correct it, but it's another to know you've done something wrong and do nothing or stay in denial. Being proactive will put you in a much better place financially and emotionally.

Paying in Full

One of the first options available to you if you haven't paid your taxes is what the IRS refers to as "paying in full." When you're behind in your taxes or haven't paid them, the IRS will always ask you to pay in full, no matter what the situation may be, although there are always extreme exceptions. For the IRS, it's the ideal situation. They immediately get all the money owed to them. I'd say it's also the ideal situation for the individual. You get it over with, move on with your life, and make better choices in the future—a one-and-done kind of thing. It's really the best option if you have the means. You'll save yourself a lot of headaches in the long run. No more stress with the IRS!

When I work with clients, the way paying in full works for most cases is I'll get a call from the IRS, because I'm acting on my client's behalf, and they'll ask me if the taxpayer can pay the full amount or not. Sometimes my clients can, so they pay in full, the IRS closes the case, and everyone moves on. But more often than not, people can't pay all the money up front, especially if they're behind in their taxes or have been living outside their means.

This is the point when people come to me for help. They want to find the best option for them or find the next best thing, other than paying in full. If this is your situation, there's no reason to feel bad or like you're in an impossible place that has no way out. Please ask for help if you need it, because that's what I'm here for. I have a Masters in Taxation degree and am well versed in tax strategies and dealing with the IRS. The worst thing you can do is pretend that everything is fine. The next thing you know, more time passes, more payments need to be collected, and more fines are handed out. This is bad even if you have the means, but it could be crippling if you don't—and it's totally avoidable. Ask for help and guidance from a professional, and you'll save money in the long run.

Paying over Time

If you can't pay in full, another option is available when it comes to paying the IRS what you owe by the deadline given in their notice (or if you know you need more time to get your funds together). An installment agreement basically tells the IRS, "Yes, I can pay this amount as adjusted, but I need more time and promise to pay in the agreed-upon timeline." Despite popular belief, it is possible to have more time to pay what you owe without being punished, if you follow IRS protocol and ask for help when you need it, in a timely manner. If you've been in the clear before, and this isn't a pattern, the IRS will usually work with you. If you have a history of not paying your taxes or not paying on time, then it probably won't work out in your favor.

An important thing to note here is that if you need more time to pay what you owe to the IRS, you can avoid extra penalties by filing your taxes by the due date, even if you know you can't pay the full amount (something many people misunderstand). If you're upfront about that and still file your taxes on time, you'll save yourself some money in the long run. This will come up again and again in this book and that's because I can't stress it enough: If you can't pay what you owe to the IRS, you still need to file your taxes on time, every year, without exception (barring extreme cases, which I'll go over later). And if you can't pay them at all or need more time to do so, then you need to be transparent and honest and communicate this with the IRS or whoever is helping you with your taxes.

The good news here is that with everything being digital now, you can apply online for a payment plan, which includes a handy installment agreement to streamline and organize the whole process for both parties. The IRS website has updates, links, and information for filing to pay over time. Fees are incurred with this, of course, but it's better than facing a penalty for not filing at all. There will also be checklists for you to determine whether you are eligible to participate in this option, along with the various methods for payment, which include direct debits and funds taken from your paycheck, among others. With all the information available on their website, the IRS makes it pretty easy to understand taxes in general and what's required of you. The language is clear, though there are a lot of intricacies, so if you want to be extra sure that you're doing everything by the book, you can always ask a professional for help.

Currently, the IRS will allow up to seventy-two months for an extension in payment time, pretty much automatically. But it's still a good idea to check the website for updates. Tax laws do change, as well as dates, timelines, fines, and fees, so it's good to continually check online to avoid any late fees or penalties. Nothing is set in stone when it comes to taxes, except that you must always pay them.

To give you a real-life example, one of my clients owed $300,000 to the IRS for a period of several years. He and his spouse filed their taxes late, and then they did some other things that they shouldn't have done with their money, which I won't get into here. Let's just say it didn't make their situation any better. Soon after, the client received an inheritance of $100,000, which, unsurprisingly, the IRS took to pay down the $300,000 they owed. The IRS also proceeded to clean out his wife's savings account of $70,000, unbeknownst to either of them. These are things the IRS has the right to do until the debt is paid, so it really doesn't make sense to live outside your means or file taxes incorrectly.

My client has paid about $170,000 of the $300,000 he owes, so to figure out what he needed to pay moving forward, and to keep him organized and accountable, I came up with a payment plan for him. I took the remaining $130,000 owed to the IRS, divided it by the 72 months, and rounded out my numbers to come up with $2,000 a month that they can reasonably pay. With those numbers and documentation, the IRS should accept that monthly amount when it comes to payment because it is reasonable and was created with the help of a professional. From that point of agreement and approval, my client will then need to make that monthly payment until all is squared away.

This is only one example, and depending on your specific situation, you may need to do a short-term payment plan instead, which is 180 days or less, or perhaps a long-term payment plan, which will last for several months. To apply online, make sure that for a long-term plan you owe less than $50,000, and for a short-term plan less than $100,000. Choosing a payment plan is always a case-by-case basis and depends on how much you are currently making, for example, and your personal situation in terms of hardship or if you have dependents. It may take a bit of time and work to clean up whatever financial situation you're in, but it's a worthy investment to gain a fresh start.

A Partial Pay Installment Agreement

Another way to pay what you owe to the IRS is by entering into a Partial Pay Installment Agreement (PPIA), which allows you to pay the IRS in installments. This option exists for cases where a person can't pay the taxes in full over seventy-two months, so applying for a PPIA offers more wiggle room. If you know you need more time to pay, keep in mind that before a PPIA will be granted, the IRS will first address your equity in assets and, if possible, use that to make payments instead of a PPIA. They will take a thorough look into your bank statements, what you own, what you make (if you're working), etc. After their assessment, if it's obvious that a full payment can't be achieved that way, then you may be able to enter into a PPIA with the IRS.

This partial payment option didn't exist until 2004, when the American Jobs Creation Act added it. A prime example of the intricacies and constantly changing nature of taxes and tax laws, a PPIA is meant to help those who need it and hopefully alleviate some stress. It's a serious agreement. If you enter into it with the IRS, not only will they take your monthly payments, but they will also monitor you to make sure all conditions are met, and they will have to approve any of your PPIAs from that point on. You will also need to fill out a full Collection Information Statement, found on the IRS website, or you can enlist the help of a professional.

Filing an Offer in Compromise

An additional option to pay the IRS is the offer in compromise (OIC), a last-resort type of agreement you may be eligible to enter into with the IRS. An OIC allows you to settle what you owe in taxes by paying less than what you owe, something many people don't even know is an option. Obviously, this is appealing for those who are in a tough spot or dealing with a less-than-ideal situation, such as owing a large amount, being out of work, or facing a life-altering emergency (the death of a spouse or a serious illness). You've probably seen ads about OICs on TV or heard about them on the radio, with promises to "settle for pennies on the dollar." However, it's important to note that if you can pay what you owe through an installment agreement, or any other way, then you won't qualify for an OIC. The IRS doesn't give them out often. It's a bad idea to lie about emergencies and dire circumstances, so always be honest about why you need an OIC.

When the IRS takes your case under consideration, if they do indeed think you have a case, they will look at your expenses, your income, and your ability to pay what you owe, and they will assert equity—basically taking stock of what you own and how much it's worth. This is a viable option for those in dire situations, such as losing your job and paying for basic necessities becomes impossible or being in the middle of a divorce and discovering that your spouse cleaned out your retirement account without your consent. The acceptance rate for an OIC is low in these cases because the IRS doesn't like to write off that kind of money, which should come as no surprise. Still, if you consult with a professional who thinks you have a chance, an OIC may be worth looking into as an option to deal with unpaid taxes. Nothing was ever lost by asking, and to wipe your slate clean of a huge debt can improve your life immensely.

Something to keep in mind, too, is that because you're relatively unlikely to win this sort of case, you should be wary of big national tax firms claiming that they can settle your liability. Such lofty statements often come by way of late-night TV advertisements, or even targeted ads in emails. But more often than not, such assertions are completely bogus. How would these large corporations have any idea of your situation and how much you owe to the IRS and when you have to pay? Don't give these firms any of your money. Go with someone trustworthy, not a conglomerate that claims to win cases without knowing what is owed or why. Word of mouth goes a long way, even in our modern times. If it sounds too good to be true, well, it probably is.

If an OIC is accepted, before entering into it, keep in mind that you will need to have filed all your tax returns (whether that's one year or several) and have made the tax payments for the year in which you're filing. If you're a business owner with employees, then you also need to have made your payroll tax deposits for the current quarter. In other words, you need to clean up all your records and make sure everything is in good shape if you want to enter into this option with the IRS, or really, for them to even consider it as an option for you. They won't be happy if your spending is all over the place, if you don't have receipts, or if you're caught in obvious lies.

The OIC, as stated earlier, is considered a last resort. In most cases, the IRS won't agree to it unless the amount you can pay is equal to or greater than what is known as the *reasonable collection potential*, which includes all your assets (cars, properties, bank accounts, and any anticipated income). They'll do a full assessment of what they think you can or can't pay, and they'll always try to use assets over an OIC. It can take a lot to get your OIC approved, but be aware that if it isn't accepted, you can file an appeal within thirty days if you don't agree with the IRS decision. Stamina and perseverance are required, but if you really need an OIC, and if you're working with a professional who agrees you have a good case, then it may be worth trying again.

The other thing that may happen when you go through this whole process is that the IRS may accept a compromise based on what is called *effective tax administration*. This means that the offer is accepted because the IRS has no doubts that the tax is owed and that the full amount can be collected; however, they also recognize that in doing so they would cause either an economic hardship or it would be unfair based on exceptional and out-of-the-ordinary circumstances.

For example, I recently submitted an effective tax administration for a client who owed about $300,000 in income taxes, with penalties and interest. Under normal circumstances, he may have had to pay in the usual fashion if his failure to pay was due to negligence, overspending, lifestyle choices, or a failed business. Around that time, though, the client was in poor health. He had suffered a stroke, and his wife now needed to take care of him. She couldn't become his caretaker and work at her job, so they lost his income and hers. While she may have collected a little bit of salary for taking care of him (not taxable, by the way), it was hardly enough to make a dent in what they owed overall. The couple suddenly found themselves in a challenging and stressful place.

They did have some equity in regard to their house, but if they needed to fix up the house or do any sort of maintenance, then they would need to use that equity. They were in a situation where we had to ask the IRS for forgiveness and a break, because they weren't doing well overall, let alone financially. These sorts of situations happen in life, and sometimes people need extra time or help. The IRS is made up of people who also go through hard times, like anyone; so, occasionally, the IRS will grant an effective tax administration. This is extremely rare, but they do understand that we all need extra help sometimes. That being said, the effective tax administration isn't something to take advantage of, or rely on, unless you're in a really dire situation—and it's best done with the help of a professional.

Currently Not Collectible

Another area you might be able to use is what is known as *currently not collectible* (CNC), a temporary status that can last for an unforeseen amount of time, such as the case with my client who had a stroke. The IRS put him in CNC status and will revisit it every so often to see if anything has changed but without a hard deadline to adhere to. As long as you don't win the Powerball or come into a huge amount of money in some surprising way, you'll be fine.

To determine your status, the IRS will balance the potential for collection of money from you against the costs and their ability to collect. They can suspend the CNC when it is deemed fair and possible; for example, if others come in to help you or you come into some unexpected funds. Economic hardship is considered as well, and the reports are made monthly to keep things up-to-date. Again, this is quite rare, but it does happen occasionally.

Bankruptcy

Another option to get rid of the taxes you owe to the IRS, primarily income tax, is filing for bankruptcy. Again, there are very strict rules here, but the idea behind bankruptcy is to help people discard debt or to make a plan to repay their debts in a way that is actually possible and not something that will last the rest of their life and into their children's or spouse's lives. The first step of bankruptcy is to file a petition with the bankruptcy court. This can be done either as an individual or with your spouse, but it can also be filed as a corporation or another entity, so bankruptcy can apply to businesses as well.

These cases are handled in federal courts, and they use rules that are outlined in the US Bankruptcy Code. A common form of bankruptcy is liquidation under Chapter 7, for those who can't make regular monthly payments toward their debt. Businesses can also file under Chapter 7. To do this, you have to be very careful and mindful that you don't incur any additional debt through this process; otherwise, the courts will view you as irresponsible or out of control, and it will only make your situation worse. If you've failed to file a return, and the IRS has filed one for you, called a *substitute for return*, those amounts cannot be discharged in bankruptcy because you did not file a return. This is something else to keep in mind so you don't get surprised. Nothing will be forgotten or discarded. You'll be in better shape if you can clear up your affairs and file everything before filing for bankruptcy.

You should be aware of other issues that surround filing for bankruptcy, such as the fact that it stays on your credit record for ten years. If you can't handle that, then you'll want to try another option. You should also know that there are taxes that can't be discharged, which applies to you if you owned a business and failed to pay the payroll taxes. If that's the case for you, then the IRS can assess you personally for what's called the *Trust Fund Recovery*

Penalty (TFRP). This serious penalty arises because the amount of money that was withheld from your employees' paychecks that you were supposed to pay to the government wouldn't be dischargeable with bankruptcy, because that is money you owed to the government. So that'll stay with you until the day you die—and even after you die, until the debt is paid.

Now that you have a better idea of what happens when you don't pay taxes, I also hope you understand more about what your options are, and what to do if you are in one of those situations. Knowledge of the situation is better than being in the dark, and if you still have questions, there are many professionals who can assist you. They've gone to school for years, and they understand the ins and outs of taxes, the law, and how to make paying off debt or fees manageable. You don't have to ruin your life over not paying taxes, and you can learn from your mistakes if you didn't file or didn't file correctly. As someone who has been in trouble with the IRS, I'm living proof that you can turn your life around and make better financial choices moving forward.

In the next chapter, we'll go over the common offenses individuals and businesses commit, some of which you may not even know are offenses, and some that are more obvious. The more you learn about what not to do, though, the more likely you will stay in good standing with the IRS, so I highly recommend paying attention and taking notes. Even if it doesn't apply to you now, it's good to know what to avoid in the future. If anyone you know is having issues or needs help, you may be able to point them in the right direction or, at the very least, comfort and encourage them to seek help from a professional.

Chapter 4

The Common Offenses

The following section contains a list of pertinent details of the most common offenses when it comes to filing, or not filing, taxes. While it's not an exhaustive list, my hope is that it will help you avoid making these mistakes. If you do make these mistakes, you'll know what's coming and how best to plan for next steps. We're all imperfect human beings, so having the wherewithal to arm yourself with knowledge and options will put you in a better place for financial success and peace of mind.

Not Filing Taxes

Perhaps the simplest of actions, or inaction, when it comes to common offenses among taxpayers is not filing their taxes. Hard to believe, what with the advent of online programs and websites. It's never been easier to file your taxes with the click of a few buttons, yet every year millions of people fail to do so. We could spend hours trying to figure out exactly why people don't file, but humans are complex and emotional beings, and so there are any number of reasons they might not file their taxes.

Some explanations are more understandable, such as experiencing a disruptive or traumatic event: a death in the family, intense medical issues, or surviving a natural disaster, such as a hurricane, fire, or flood, that causes you to lose all tax and financial records. These are serious and understandable reasons to not file taxes, what I would refer to as legitimate reasons. When you're going through any of these sorts of issues or events, you may be in survival mode and just trying to get through each day in one piece. You might not have the documents you need for reasons out of your control. The IRS understands that and can forgive those cases, despite the common perception that they only care about money and have no room for sympathy or second chances.

Outside of the aforementioned legitimate reasons, though, there are other less legitimate reasons that people don't want to file taxes. Perhaps they think they don't have to file if they pay for everything with cash, or perhaps they're mad at the government and don't think it's fair that they have to pay for things they don't use, like highways, or don't agree with, like the military. They hope they won't get caught because they don't have an obvious paper trail or forms that can be traced and lined up. This, by the way, is an offense that happens with both individuals and businesses, which are big no-nos.

There are also some people who don't want to be in the IRS system, or any system at all. There are others who do agree with and understand taxes, but a year or more has passed without them filing, for whatever reason, and now they don't know how to get back into the system without calling attention to themselves. They worry that filing will cause more trouble than is reasonable. In those cases, some people might have already gone years without filing a tax return and now think that it's too late or that they're a lost cause. They feel shame, so they choose to avoid the problem rather than deal with it. Meanwhile, those letters and notices keep piling up in a way that makes everything worse.

The next thing you know, you may want to or need to file a tax return because you're getting married and want to buy a house. The bank is going to ask for copies of your tax return to obtain a loan. That's when people get really scared and start doing things that don't make sense or make their situation worse. They're afraid that the IRS is going to see what they've been up to. In the case of a business, the IRS will wonder how a brand-new business is making $500,000 a year, for example. It's a legitimate question. On top of that, the business doesn't have any tax returns on file, which isn't good for anyone.

It all feels like a huge problem, and some people let it go on and on. It just keeps snowballing and getting worse until they reach a point of panic. Now instead of five years of returns to file, they might have seven or eight years of returns to file, which would overwhelm anyone. In a few cases, I've had people who hadn't filed for decades. They came to see me because of impending marriage, wanting to buy property, or simply having a guilty conscience. I question why they didn't come sooner, but late is better than never.

No matter how bad you think your situation is, it would be much worse to have the IRS knocking at your door, asking why you haven't filed your taxes, and then putting a lien on whatever you own. From there, you may have to refinance your mortgage, and guess what? You can't, because the IRS has a lien on it. So that means you need to file your taxes to get the lien released. This is just one example, but you'd be surprised how easily people fall into a trap they can't get out of. Everything goes back to filing the taxes, so if you are past due, stop here and file your taxes before you do anything else. If you're in a bad situation, one that is involved, complex, and has gone on for many years, ask someone with knowledge of the IRS and taxes to help you. Believe me, you'll be glad you did, and it will bring you much peace of mind.

Trying to Hide Income

Another common way people get in trouble with the IRS is by trying to hide their income, thinking they can pull a fast one because the IRS won't check if everything matches up or not. This seems to happen most often when people with a business ask their customers or clients to pay them in cash so that there's no digital paper trail, as you might have with checks or credit cards. To further incentivize clients to pay in cash, business owners might offer a discount, or an extra bonus, or a free item or service. For example, I had a client who decided that he was going to report only what was deposited in the bank through credit card transactions and checks, but not any of the cash he received, which was around one-third of what he reported. The IRS found out, and he went to prison, in addition to having to pay the taxes, penalties, and interest.

People have also used services like PayPal and Venmo to get around using credit cards and then using those statements as a way to pay fewer taxes or no taxes. It's getting more difficult to do that now, though, with the recent changes in the laws because of an uptick in digital services. This is another reason to keep up with the IRS website or use a professional to help you when it comes to filing taxes to make sure everything is by the book. Ten years ago, we wouldn't think about this so much, if at all, but now credit card companies and services like PayPal, Venmo, and Zelle are required to send out reporting forms to their customers, a 1099-K. These forms state that if your transactions total $600 or more during the year, they will notify you and the IRS, and you need to pay taxes on those amounts.

If you do everything through Venmo, for example, then the 1099-K from Venmo better match up with what you report on your 1040, or you're going to have a problem. You don't want to ignore these notices or forms, or try to put numbers that don't match, because those big companies are definitely going to send what they need to send to the IRS. They don't want to get in trouble, so you need to make sure you keep up your end of the deal as well. Keep it simple. Report all the income you make, fill out the proper forms, and you should be fine. You'll gain nothing from trying to hide income from the IRS. Report your income, and in the long run, you'll actually save money.

Accurately reporting your income is especially important for those who work in the gig economy: freelancers, independent contractors, and anyone else who is self-employed. You have to keep up with your invoices, sure, but you also have to keep up with your forms. Your line of work may require more IRS forms to keep track of because you're interacting with clients who use different payment methods. With all your forms in place, when it comes time to file, you won't have to scramble, you won't miss any funds or write-offs, and you'll remain in good standing with the IRS. Nobody wants a headache from dealing with the IRS, and nobody wants to pay unnecessary fees.

Bartering

Another area that people often miss, or don't account for, when it comes to filing is bartering. Bartering has to be reported. There are formal barter exchanges that send out 1099s for transactions, which takes the guesswork out of it. So, for example, if you write a book for someone in exchange for them doing your taxes, and neither party reports any income from the exchange, that's technically hiding income from the IRS. Not something you should do. Help yourself and join the formal bartering systems that exist for this sort of work and income, such as the Barter Business Exchange in North Carolina. A quick search on the internet can probably find you a local chapter.

The North Carolina chapter is just one example of a network of business owners who help each other prosper by trading products and services within their communities to increase commerce and reduce cash expenditures. They have around a thousand active business listings, which is nothing to sneeze at, and goes to show that bartering is a service many want to and do participate in. So, to go back to the original example I gave, if I did someone's tax return, and we were both on the exchange, then I would get 700 credits for doing their tax return. If I wanted to, I could then use those 700 credits to go to Joe's Butcher Shop and buy a bunch of steaks, or go to Anna's Sports Store and buy some products for scuba diving.

Either way, if you aren't on a formal or official bartering network, you'll have to figure out how much your service would have cost, and what you got in return. Then you'll need to get some sort of official document, even if it's an invoice, so that you have something you could point to if for some reason the IRS audits you.

Using Someone as a Conduit

Another common offense that people commit is using somebody else as a conduit or an alter ego, what is also referred to as a *straw man*. For example, I could tell my client to make a check out to my son for something, and then my son would go ahead and use that money to pay for something personal for me, such as my mortgage payment, because I told him to. The money wasn't for his use—it was always meant for me—but by making out the check to someone else, the money wouldn't be taxed in the same way or be viewed as something that I spent money on. That's willfully lying, or trying to deceive the IRS, and they don't take kindly to that.

People will also sometimes make up whole corporations, when really the individual is providing the service or product. And then, depending on the set up, the person can take money out of the corporation as a loan, and then the business fails to file a business tax return. This is another way to get in trouble with the IRS, so the message is the same in either case: Be truthful about how you earn and spend your money. Don't make up people or positions that don't exist, and you should be okay.

Not Claiming Income from Illegal Activities

Some people may not realize this, but not claiming income from illegal activities is exactly how Al Capone got convicted. To be more specific, he didn't file a tax return. After a life of crime, and after being involved in so many illegal activities and deaths and shady businesses, he was caught because he didn't file his taxes. Talk about a clear warning that nobody is above the law, at least when it comes to filing taxes. Believe it or not, there are actual laws on the books that lay out what you can deduct against income from selling drugs, engaging in sex work, and committing other forms of illicit activities.

Because cannabis is still illegal on the federal level but is quickly changing on the state level, there's a great need for accountants on the state and local levels to help determine how to tax income and expenditures. When dealing in these sorts of products, it's just as important to know what you can deduct, what you can't deduct, and how to report things the correct way to make sure you stay within the federal law (until it becomes legal, that is).

Despite what people think, sex workers and thieves absolutely need to report their income too. When I was in college, one of my professors, a lawyer, told us a story about some bank robbers who came into his office. They spoke openly and asked him all sorts of questions about whether they had to report the income they got from robbing banks and if they could deduct the pistols and other weapons they had purchased as business equipment.

It says a lot that individuals who were robbing banks weren't scared to get caught by the police, but they were scared to get caught by the IRS for not filing their taxes correctly. They could have felt this way because the IRS is forbidden from sharing information about what you file, or what you do in general, with other agencies such as the FBI or CIA. Unless the IRS gets a subpoena, they aren't going to report you for illegal activities like robbing banks or selling drugs. As a CPA, I must adhere to the guidelines of Circular 230, a treasury publication that outlines all the rules and requirements for tax breaks and people who represent clients before the IRS.

Legally, there's certain things I can't do, like turn a client in for crimes. It's kind of like attorney-client privilege, and we take it seriously. We're not here to bust clients for what they do in their lives; our job is to help them with their taxes. I'm certainly not one to judge what others do. The only thing I can judge is if you don't have your taxes· in order and you don't ask for help. For me, if you're in my office or on the phone asking for assistance, you're on the right path. Bottom line is, you should always follow the tax laws, even if you're not following the other laws.

Filing Fraudulent Tax Returns

Another common offense I have run into are situations where married people file as single people so that one or both of the spouses can get the Earned Income Tax Credit (EITC). This is illegal because married people have only two ways to file a return: jointly or separately. To do anything else is a huge no-no. People, unfortunately, get into these situations, and sometimes they get there by not-so-well-meaning tax preparers. The preparers want to make more money, and by getting their clients more money, they can charge more for their services. But that's a lose-lose situation if you get audited. If you work with a preparer, be sure to read the reviews or use someone who comes recommended.

There are also quite a few people who try to "rent" their kids to somebody else so that they can use them as dependents to get the various credits that are available to people who have kids. The EITC is something that Congress enacted, and it states that if you have dependents, and you make under a certain dollar amount, depending on the number of dependents you have and that dollar amount, you can get more money back than you paid into the system. Congress created the credit to help those who are supporting a lot of people. Unfortunately, some individuals take advantage of the opportunity.

For example, if I wanted to game the system, and I didn't have a job, but I did have three kids, the EITC wouldn't do me any good. What I could do instead would be to let someone else I knew, say a friend or relative, claim my three kids in exchange for $1,000 of the $4,000 refund that I would normally get if I had a job. That way, without doing anything, I could make money, and so could my co-conspirator. But, of course, the IRS will check on this, and they'll send you a letter asking you to substantiate that these three kids lived with you—through a landlord letter, rent agreement, doctors' records, or school records, things like that—which show that they were your legal dependents.

I personally haven't run into a lot of this because that's not the level of clients that we work with at my company, but it is somewhat prevalent. People who claim the EITC are probably the most heavily audited in the country. It has become a big problem in the United States, so the IRS is on high alert to check into the validity of the claims for child income credits. It isn't fun to have to pay the fines for that or face possible prison time. If you have kids and don't have a job, try your best to find a job. I understand there are times when finding a job is nearly impossible, such as during a pandemic, but lying and cheating the IRS isn't the smart way to go.

I work more often in areas that involve fraudulent returns. I represented a client once in an audit, and it turned out his tax preparer had made up a phony business. Not only that, the tax preparer then put it on a Schedule C and claimed that my client had made a little bit of income from that. But the tax preparer didn't stop there. He also created all kinds of false expenses for this false business. In this case, both the taxpayer and the tax preparer knew what they were doing—cheating the system—and as you may have gathered by now, the IRS doesn't take too kindly to that.

To be fair, this client actually did own a small business, but it was nothing like what the tax preparer had presented on the forms in terms of what was being spent and earned. So when it came time to substantiate the expenses, the client couldn't, and that's where everything really fell apart. You must back everything up and have documents ready to prove how you make and spend your money. If you don't have that information, you'll have a lot of problems in your future. My client wasn't too happy that he now owed another $10,000 or $15,000 in taxes due to the fines and penalties. As I stated earlier, it doesn't pay to use the government as a bank. This sort of thing happens more frequently than you might think, and while I can help people lower the fines and taxes, I can't make them magically disappear. Do your best to be honest and therefore avoid any mess.

Taking Deductions You're Not Entitled To

Claiming dependents that aren't yours falls under this next category: taking deductions you're not entitled to.

Other areas would be making up a phony business, per the example I gave in the last section, and taking charitable contributions that you didn't make. The latter isn't really an issue now, but it was back in the day when you could itemize deductions. I've seen some wild things happen when it comes to this offense, and though it's not common, I do occasionally get some strange stories. Once I got a call from a woman somewhere in Tennessee; she told me that her son was in prison in Wisconsin, and he was getting close to the tax filing deadline. She was calling because she wanted to see if I could file a tax return for him, and I said I would.

When I asked how she found me, she said her son was at the Columbia Correctional Institution in Portage, Wisconsin, and one day he was sitting around the prison yard and a fellow inmate asked him if he had filed his taxes yet. When he said no, the guy said, "You should call Jon Neal. He's really good at filing taxes." (I'm not sure if I knew the inmate, or maybe I knew someone he knew, but either way, I was recommended.) This was a long time ago, by the way, before my own issues with the IRS.

The son and mother sent all the information to me. This guy had a bunch of 1099s from casinos for amounts like $500,000, and he claimed that they withheld something astronomical like $200,000 in taxes. He also had letters from charities he had supposedly donated to. They looked real to me, but I passed them around the office anyway because something felt off. Everyone agreed that they looked real, so I gave him the benefit of the doubt. I had no reason not to believe him, and he had documentation, which most people who lie don't have.

This was around the time of 9/11, or pretty soon after, and the inmate had a letter from the Red Cross thanking him for his generous donation of $150,000 to the survivors of 9/11 in New York City. It had the official Red Cross logo, it was signed, and like I said, it looked legit. I went ahead and attached everything to the return for full disclosure, if you will, and after all that, it looked like he was getting a $110,000 refund from the IRS. A few months later, two guys carrying guns and badges came into my office and asked, "Did you do the return for this man?" I said yes, gave them the whole story, and pulled out the file where I had attached all the supporting documentation.

It turned out that the man wanted to be transferred to the federal prison system instead of the state prison system because he thought they had better food and better accommodations. He filed the fraudulent tax return to claim deductions he wasn't entitled to, and he had done this for two years before me. This was an instance where the person was convincing. Other times, it's obvious that people are making up their numbers and support, especially when you see handwritten sheets of expenses, numbers that make no sense, or weird expenses. It's most obvious when there's no documentation at all.

☑

Before closing this chapter, I'd like to leave you with a final note. Up until 2017, if you were single, the standard deduction was around $6,000. If you were married, it was around $12,000, and there was no limitation on how much you could deduct for state and local taxes. But when Congress scrapped these rates under President Donald Trump, they basically said, "We're going to raise the standard deduction for a single person to $12,000, and we're going to raise the standard deduction for a married couple to $24,000. We're also going to limit your deduction for state or local income taxes, or actually state and local taxes, to $10,000." So where maybe around 40 percent of people who filed tax returns took the standard deduction in the past, that number is now up to about 85 percent, all because they raised the standard deduction, and they restricted some of your deductions for taxes. As a result, taxpayers who had high real estate taxes on their homes were limited in their deduction, as were those with job-related expenses, such as unreimbursed mileage, since those are no longer deductible.

After reading about the common offenses, you should, at the very least, feel more inclined to always file your taxes on time, not cheat on them, and make sure to work with a professional who has a good reputation. Most people aren't in a really bad situation, and their issues have occurred only out of neglect and ignorance of the rules. If you're in a tough situation, I highly recommend getting someone to help you out. Avoiding fines and fees, and especially going to prison, is something you'll want help with—believe me. In the next chapter, I'll cover some of the common penalties, another area to be aware of when it comes to taxes.

Chapter 5

The Common Penalties

If you already know you're in a bad place when it comes to filing taxes because you did something illegal or wrong, or you know you're going to have some issues with the IRS, then you'll want to take note of what penalties may come to pass. Even if you're not in trouble, it's still good to be informed about what might happen and what to do if you or the business you run is in trouble in any way. You don't want to find yourself in a situation where you're desperate or scared, and then a tough situation becomes even tougher.

The good news is, if you have done something that warrants a charge or penalty, the IRS will let you know. It's not like they'll keep it from you until the last moment. They'll send a notice or letter to tell you about the penalty you're being charged with or the offense you're being accused of, and then they'll go into details about the reason for the charge and what you need to do next. This is good because they take the guesswork out of it and provide you with an identification number for your specific case.

That being said, as with anything from the IRS, don't blindly accept the charge. Double-check that the numbers and information are correct. As I stated earlier, the IRS makes mistakes. You need to investigate that first letter and possibly save yourself time and money. Don't do it further down the road, and don't do nothing at all. Remember, too, that the IRS website has more information to help you understand your notice or letter, or you can hire a professional to walk you through it, step-by-step.

Substantial Understatement Penalty

When it comes to negligence or an understatement of income, the IRS will charge an Accuracy-Related Penalty, which amounts to 20 percent of whatever you underpaid for your taxes, or basically whatever you still owe them. This is only for individuals, and it only comes into play if you understate your tax liability. In terms of businesses, if you claim a Section 199A Qualified Business Income Deduction, you can still be penalized if you understate the tax liability. The best way to know what you will, and should, be charged with regarding these penalties is to check back often on the IRS website. It will also help if you keep good, accurate, and up-to-date records.

As far as tax returns go with businesses, including those who are self-employed, if you fail to file a partnership return or an S corporation tax return, then there's a per partner, or per shareholder, per month penalty you will be responsible for. If you fail to file an income tax return within sixty days of the due date as extended to you, then there's another penalty for that, and that amount changes depending on the year. Make sure to check the IRS website for details to know what you owe. Check it more than once, and have others check the numbers for you as well.

There are also penalties for corporations and individuals who do not pay either 90 percent of this year's tax liability or 100 percent, or 110 percent of the previous year's liability through withholding or quarterly estimated tax payments. Corporations and individuals face a penalty for failure to file a tax return, failure to file on time, as well as an additional penalty for failure to pay on time. These penalties can go up to 50 percent of the tax that's due. All the more reason to pay what you owe initially, rather than underpay and incur penalties and fines that make everything more stressful.

Finally, there's also a penalty for what the IRS calls negligence, material misstatement, and underreporting of income. So if what you report is less than 80 percent of your income, the IRS can charge businesses and individuals a Civil Fraud Penalty that amounts to 100 percent of the tax that's due. The lessons here, as always, are to be honest, be on time, and when needed, get some professionals in your corner.

Civil Fraud

Another area in which people find themselves in trouble is civil fraud, or when you file a return in bad faith. Basically, it's when you, the taxpayer, know that the return is false, and you file a false return to evade paying the proper tax liability. You knew that the information was incorrect, but you did it anyway, which is something else the IRS is not a fan of. By the way, you may be alarmed to find out (but it's great to know) that there is no statute of limitations on the IRS auditing you if they suspect fraud and can prove fraud.

The IRS can go as far back as they like, and those numbers will add up if they're looking at more than a few years or, in extreme cases, decades. They'll charge you with civil fraud penalties when there is clear and convincing evidence to prove that you committed fraud. They will need to show that you purposefully intended to evade paying taxes, or fewer taxes, and you knew what you were doing. The key here is intent—knowing that what you were doing was wrong and doing it anyway. So if you were even thinking about filing an incorrect return, or wondering if the IRS really does punish people for this, don't do it, and yes, they most certainly do.

Two more things to keep in mind regarding fraud. One, if you file with a spouse, only one spouse can be fined with fraud, unless it seems that both parties knowingly participated in the fraud. Two, the IRS understands that there's a huge difference between intent and making an honest mistake. You might have paid less because of bad advice, a difference of opinion, carelessness, or some other forgivable reason.

If you get a notice from the IRS, make sure to send your information to the place indicated in the notice to avoid anything getting lost or delayed. This may seem simple and obvious, but remember, every day that you don't pay, you will be charged more, and those fees can add up.

Filing Late Taxes

Something many people might not know or think about is that if you have late taxes, you should file them now to limit the interest charges and late payment fees. Maybe that seems strange, especially if you don't have the money to pay what you owe, but it's best to file the taxes now and get yourself out of an avoidable hole. It all starts with filing taxes, and the best advice I can give people is to file them on time, even if you know you can't pay them. If you're beyond that, then file those past due returns right now, the same way and in the same place you normally would. If you need help, ask for it. Don't hide from filing your taxes; otherwise, those penalties will just keep growing.

Another reason to file the return is that if you don't, you might miss out on the refund that is yours to have and should be collected. You must file your return and claim the refund within three years of the return due date, which also applies to tax credits like the EITC. It really does expire, so don't let that money disappear. For people who are self-employed, if you don't file the return, you won't get credits toward Social Security retirement or disability benefits. That maybe doesn't seem to matter much now, especially if you're young, but it will matter when you don't work anymore and still need to support yourself or your family and take care of health care and other needs.

What's more, if you're applying for loans or need to in the future, the approvals might get delayed if you don't file your tax return on time. You might need a loan for a mortgage, for a business, or for school. So again, these are more reasons to file and pay on time, as much as you are able. If you do indeed owe more than you can pay to the IRS, you can ask for an extension of between 60 and 120 days. We went over this in the section on installment payments and the offer in compromise, and this is a reminder that there are usually more options out there for taxpayers than they realize.

Failure to Pay Estimated Taxes

You will incur a penalty from the IRS if you don't pay your estimated tax on your income or you pay it late, which relates to the previous section. This can warrant a penalty, even if the IRS owes you a refund, so don't think that will exempt you. This is also known as the *Underpayment of Estimated Tax by Individuals Penalty*. To put it simply, the IRS will come up with the penalty based on the amount you underpaid, when those amounts were due and underpaid, as well as the interest rate on the underpayments (charged quarterly). This can add up quickly and make a huge dent in your funds.

You can dispute a penalty if you have a reasonable cause to show you didn't underpay, or if you were given incorrect advice from a professional, or if you followed the advice of the IRS that was stated in the notice you were sent and were still penalized. You'll have to mail a statement to them alerting them to their error, signed and under the penalty of perjury, so only do that if you're sure the dispute is reasonable and true.

Payroll Tax Penalties

Another area in which some people incur penalties from the IRS, and the one that is most personal to me and my story, are payroll tax penalties. The punishment for this is on the more serious side, as it involves more than one person—namely, your employees, of which you could have hundreds, thousands, or more. What happens in this case is that the IRS will implement penalties and interest on employers when they don't collect, report, or remit payroll taxes. If you are the employer in that situation, you can be held personally responsible for any errors when it comes to those items. Even if you outsourced that role to a payroll service or a bookkeeper, you are still the person who will be held responsible. This is yet another reason you want to make sure you do it yourself or, if you don't have the time or you have too many employees, use someone who is both professional and known for their accuracy.

An area that many people get in trouble with is the penalties that come from failing to make the deposits for payroll on a timely basis or not making them at all. And while there are many requirements and penalties that are listed online at the IRS website, there are some that are more common, such as Form 941, which is when you are withholding income, Social Security, and Medicare taxes. The other common occurrence is the failure to provide information forms like W-2s and the 1099-NECs to employees and independent contractors, which is how they get their Social Security benefits, 401(k)s, health care, and more. How much you will have to pay in penalties may depend on how big your company is, the types of error(s) you made, and how late the payment was made, if you have even paid it.

If you are required to make deposits, such as payments of payroll taxes through an electronic filing system, you can face a penalty for not using the proper payment method. You might send in the payments via check versus doing it electronically, when electronically (via the Electronic Federal Tax Payment System) is required for most employers.

And then, of course, there's a criminal penalty for failure to withhold payroll taxes, which is what I was convicted for and is certainly a situation no person wants to be in. There is also a penalty for not paying payroll taxes when they are due, the TFRP I referred to earlier. As I mentioned, what this means is that you may have withheld the Social Security, income tax, or Medicare taxes from your employees' pay but didn't have them remitted or set aside for the government. Employers are legally required to do so, no matter what area of business and no matter how small or large the business is. This penalty cannot be discharged in bankruptcy.

As the owner of a company, or anyone the IRS considers a responsible person, you have the legal responsibility of paying these payroll taxes to the IRS. If you don't pay them when they are due and in the right amount, the IRS can charge the individual with a TFRP, which is 100 percent of what was withheld from employee paychecks. That becomes your personal responsibility, and it will stay with you forever—and that is not an exaggeration. Stealing from the government is not taken lightly, and the TFRP requires a willful failure to take action. Even so, you might still get fined even if you can prove the failure to pay or report the taxes wasn't intentional. You will get fined for late payments, and depending on the number of employees you have, it could very well be a large amount.

What I Learned from My Experience

The most obvious thing I learned from my own experiences is to always, always pay your payroll taxes on time and in the right amount if you are an employer and are responsible for other people's salaries. It's your legal responsibility, and it's an area that the IRS is often on the lookout for; they will notice if something is not matching up. If you're lucky (though, really, not lucky at all), then maybe they won't catch you right away, such was the case in my situation, but eventually they will catch you. If you're tempted to deceive, or have thought about it, learn a big lesson from me and just don't.

I got away with not paying the payroll taxes for a few years, but then the day came where two agents with badges and guns knocked on my door. It's not worth the risk, nor the money and possible destruction of your life. It's not worth wondering when you will get caught and having to lie to the people around you. It's not worth the time and energy. I understand the shame around failing in business, or needing help, but it's always better to fail in that sense than try to cheat the IRS. We all make mistakes, and we all get in situations where it's better to admit defeat—that's part of being human. To stay in denial will hurt you, sure, but it also hurts others.

Since my conviction, I'm happy to say that I've always paid my taxes and the payroll taxes in the right amounts. I've been late in my payments a time or two, but I paid those penalties and got it all squared away in a timely fashion. The truth is that if you treat the government like a money lender and hold on to their money for too long, they're going to charge you for it, and they're a very expensive lender. You don't want to borrow from the government—take it from me. They weren't meant to act as banks for taxpayers, and they don't take too kindly to late payments or failure to pay.

My entire experience of being found out by the IRS, to being able to work again, to being back in good standing, lasted almost four years. That was the amount of time it took for the IRS to go through my records and come up with the charges, then determine when and how I had to pay everything back, and whether I would need to serve time for the felony charge. While they were doing that, though, I kept on working and keeping my nose clean and hoping for the best, but I also wasn't being too optimistic, because I knew what I had done was serious. Eventually, I was charged, convicted, sent to prison, served time, released, on probation, and finally allowed to practice again.

In a way, it was a relief to not have this secret anymore. I always knew in the back of my mind that the moment might come when I would be found out—and it could come when I was least expecting it. Though, in a way, I was always expecting it. You can't do what I was doing for long and rest easy. The not knowing was the worst part for me, so at least I knew I didn't have to pretend anymore and could start to make up for my mistakes. It wouldn't be fun or easy, but at least I would have a plan and know what I had to do to get back in good standing with the

IRS, my employees, my friends, my family, and, of course, with myself.

The penalty I incurred, the Failure to Deposit Penalty, applies to employers like me who don't make employment tax deposits on time, in the right amount, or in the right way. This includes Social Security, Medicare taxes, and Federal Unemployment Tax, which employers are supposed to send to the IRS either quarterly, monthly, or semiweekly. As I said, I knowingly didn't do this, and so the penalty was based on the number of days the deposits were late, which in my case was many years.

The thing to stress here is that the IRS is aggressive when it comes to this sort of matter. If you don't pay the government, they'll think you're stealing their money, which, in essence, is what I was doing. And no one likes to be stolen from. If you have a lot of employees in your business, those payroll taxes really do add up, and the penalty against the person responsible, like me, can be huge. It can mean thousands of dollars or more, and it can mean prison time. It can disrupt your entire life, and the lives of those closest to you.

While it's not always the case that failing to pay these taxes can lead to criminal charges, it did in my situation. It's a felony, punishable by up to $10,000, or up to five years in prison, or both. You'll get charged more harshly if you use the money you withhold from the government for your own personal use, like to fund vacations, fix up a house, or buy cars, versus using the funds to pay creditors or keeping other businesses afloat, which is what I did. I thought it would be a one-time thing, a quick fix, until I could get the businesses in good standing, and then I would pay the money back. Wishful thinking, of course, and not a great thing to do, even with the best of intentions. Still, spending five months in prison was better than five years, so it could have been much worse.

Some of the people I worked with at the time suspected something was up, and then when the agents came into the office, they knew for sure. But my family had no idea, not even my wife. I was trying to keep it all secret, hoping that things would pan out, that I would get lucky and get back the money I had used, and that nobody would notice. It's often hardest to tell the people closest to you when you've made a mistake, but it was wrong of me to hide it from them.

The reaction at home when my family found out was not good, which probably comes as no surprise. My wife was furious with me, as she had every right to be. Had she known earlier, she might not have been so upset, but not finding out until the IRS agents came to my office made her very unhappy with me. I'm lucky she stood by me through it all, and I won't ever forget that. I'm grateful that she could see that I had made a few bad choices and that it didn't make me a bad person.

We all make mistakes, and sometimes it gets worse before it gets better. The important thing I've learned from this experience is that it's one thing to make a mistake, but it's another to take ownership of it and put in the hard work to correct your errors. It's not enough to pay the penalties and fines and go to prison—you must be committed to growing and being better in the future. That's a long-lasting change, and for that I am also grateful. I can honestly say I'm a better CPA and person now. I have more empathy and a stronger sense of boundaries and limits on risky behavior.

I won't go into too many details about my experience of going to prison and being in that environment, but I can say that you certainly meet a lot of interesting people from all walks of life. Some of the people I met were guys who worked at well-known, high-priced New York law firms, guys who seemed to have it all and then were convicted of drug charges. I also met people who had already spent twenty-five years in the prison system for a relatively minor offense, for things that they might not get charged with today, like marijuana possession with no previous charges. It was an interesting experience and very humbling. You get a lot of time to think when you're in prison, and I have to say that it made me appreciate all the things and people I had in my life more than ever.

I was lucky overall because I was only in prison for a short amount of time. Five months may seem like a long time when you're going in or thinking about it in the abstract sense, but when I got out, it felt like the time had passed quickly. My family supported me the entire way, and when I got out, they were there, standing by my side.

Most of the people in my office that I worked with at that time are still working for me now, which I am also appreciative of. That's not to say that everyone was supportive; a few of my old employees did jump ship and spread the news about my predicament when it happened, purposefully trying to make me look bad.

Because of my bad decisions, The Neal Group lost around 40 percent of our business, but I'm happy to say that we built it back and are doing well now. That should be clear proof that it is possible to come back from bad decisions when it comes to paying (or not paying) taxes and that you can build your life back in a better way. Even when a situation feels really dire, it can get better. And if you think that's cliché, well, I'm living proof of it. I'm living proof that not all people will disown you and that you can get your life back on track, both personally and professionally

When I got out of prison, I was put on extended supervision, what used to be called probation. I suppose the government wanted something a little softer sounding. The United States probate office of supervision monitored me, which basically meant I could go to work and come home, and nothing else for about a year. My freedom of movement was restricted; I was being watched to make sure I didn't do anything else illegal and was staying away from temptation and trouble.

I'm sure that some people go back to their old ways and need to be monitored, which is also why when you're under extended supervision, you're not allowed to be friends with or associate with people who are criminals or will knowingly commit a crime. This is probably a good rule of thumb regardless, but if you have committed a crime, it makes sense to not be around that kind of influence. It's always better to stick to home and work. Of course, it's hard to predict what people are going to do. If you know good people who don't get in trouble, then that's who you should surround yourself with.

When I did have to go to other places outside of my office and home, I had to follow a strict set of rules. Every time I went to see clients somewhere other than my office, I had to write it down on a sheet, outlining where I went, how many miles it was, and what day it was. I had to send those over to my probation officer every week, to have a paper trail of where I was, who I was with, when I was with them, and why. A lack of freedom of movement is something most of us take for granted, and believe me, it doesn't feel great to have to account for every move you make, especially if it's for work or family.

Another humbling thing I had to do during this time was wear an ankle monitor. I had that thing on for about two years. I wouldn't wish that on anyone, because again, it represents your lack of freedom and is a constant reminder of what you did wrong. In our day-to-day lives, most of us don't think about how nice it is to go to the grocery store or go for a walk around the block. For me, I had to think about and document every move.

There are other rules and regulations that came with being under supervision. If I had to go out of town, I couldn't just document it or ask my probation officer for permission. I had to undergo a whole official process and petition a judge. I remember one time I did exactly that to attend a seminar in St. Louis. During the seminar, a man from the probation office called me (they have people working twenty-four hours a day who monitor your whereabouts, by the way), saying that my ankle monitor showed that I wasn't at home. He asked me where I was, and I said I was in St. Louis for a seminar. He asked me who told me I could go there, and I told him that the judge who was involved in my case had granted me permission and that I was in possession of the letter granting said permission. I let him know that he should have a copy as well. I heard him rummaging around a bit, in typical government bureaucracy fashion, until he finally found the paper and said everything was fine and to have a good night. This was not an uncommon occurrence, and I always made sure to have my documentation in order.

After those first couple of years, the probation office eased up on me, and as long as I told them ahead of time where I was planning to go and when I was going, they were okay with it. All I would have to do was email my probation officer and tell her the truth, like, "I have to go down to Chicago on Tuesday to pick up my daughter from the O'Hare airport. I'll be leaving at eight o'clock and should be back by noon." Or I might tell her something like, "I'm going to be in St. Louis because my son's wife is having her first child, and I don't know when this is going to happen, but that's where I'll be." By that point, my probation officer was comfortable enough with me to trust that I wasn't trying to put anything over on her. I never had any issues with her, and it was a relief to have to deal with less paperwork and less skepticism, though I still didn't have all my freedoms back.

As I mentioned earlier, another huge part of the consequence of my mistakes was that I lost my CPA license. I lost my privilege to practice before the Internal Revenue Service, but once I got my CPA license back, then I could apply to practice before the IRS again. I had to go through the whole process to get back my CPA license, and I think it took about a year to do that, and then it took another three years to get reinstated and be able to practice before the IRS. During that time, I couldn't talk to the IRS or help any taxpayer with tax issues. Normally, though, it takes about five years to practice again, so I was pleased. It felt good to be working and to be back in good standing, not only with the IRS, but also with my employees, my community, and of course, my family.

The last thing I'm required to do and what I'm working on now, the last part of the puzzle, is paying restitution. I'm happy to report that I'm close to paying it all off. When I have, I can truly continue with a clean slate. It's been a long road, and I wouldn't make the same mistakes twice. In the end, I hope you can take a cue from me and not make the same mistakes I did. It really doesn't make sense to cheat the IRS, and even less so if you're an employer. That's an area they are extra vigilant with, and sooner or later, you will get caught. No amount of money is worth that, and no good intentions will lessen the punishment you receive.

If you've done something like what I did, my best advice is to pay off what you can now and not make the situation worse. Don't continue down the path you started, because it won't get better, and it won't undo what you've already done. Ask for help and call a professional who is known for being honest and fair, with good reviews and a clean track record. Not paying payroll taxes, as you now know, is a felony, so you want someone who knows how to prepare for that. It may look bad, but a trained expert can help, and it's never too late to turn things around. Look at me. I'm the perfect example of someone who made a mistake—or many—and was able to rebuild their life. If that doesn't give you hope, well, I don't know what will.

Chapter 6

Strategies and Best Practices for Success

I wrote this book because I wanted to show people that everybody is human, and if you make mistakes, you can correct those mistakes. One of the simplest and easiest things you can do as a taxpayer, aside from paying your taxes, is to not ignore letters from the IRS or the state. If you get a letter from either of these entities, open it right away. Don't think that it will go away, because it won't. Wishful thinking will get you nowhere, and you have to be prepared to face whatever the contents say. Waiting and pretending the letter doesn't exist will only make the fines steeper and your stress greater.

To illustrate this point, I'll tell you a bit about a client I was recently working with. He owed more than $50,000 to the IRS, and because of that, he had his passport revoked and couldn't leave the country. On top of that, he hadn't realized that the IRS had also taken $80,000 out of his bank account. Why didn't he know? Because he never bothered to open the letters they sent to him, which, as I've said several times, is one of the most important and easiest things to do. Still, people freeze up at those letters and let their fears get the best of them.

Once we opened them together, it turned out that he had received certified letters from the IRS that said they were going to take money out of his bank account. When the IRS says they're going to do something, they do it. That was when he came to talk to me and let me know that he needed to file his tax returns and work out a payment plan. My response was that it was a little late for all that, but it wasn't impossible to get him out of a tough situation. I helped him get squared away with the IRS, and then my work was to double back and try and get some of the penalties revoked for him. It was a messy case, but certainly not the worst case I've ever seen.

Make Sure Your Information Is Correct

Aside from paying your taxes when they're due, and not ignoring the IRS's official letters, it's always a good idea to ask for assistance to make sure that all your information is correct on your forms. I'm not saying you should always get help or that everyone should spend money on that, but when you need a professional, it's best to get one who knows what's going on and can save you time and anxiety. You may also feel more relaxed if that person has gone through what you're going through, a reason a lot of people feel comfortable with me. I'm by no means perfect. I don't try to pretend that I've never done anything wrong in my life. I'm open about it, and also, I really do want to help people not do what I did.

You may not know everything that is deductible. A professional should ask questions about your situation so you can minimize your taxes. Questions about dependents, college tuition, medical expenses, and retirement plans often result in tax savings immediately or in the future.

One time, I had a guy who came to me after he got out of prison himself. We compared notes about where we were and what we experienced, and I could tell he felt at ease with me. Part of that, too, is that my clients can tell that I don't judge them—I'm here to help them, no matter what. That client wrote me a five-star review on Google. It goes to show that when you're good at your job and relate to people on their level, they'll show you appreciation and go out of their way to spread the word. It's easy for me to treat people with respect and to listen to their needs. That goes a long way in this business that deals with money. It's worked well so far, and I have no plans on changing my approach.

Use Good Business Principles

A best practice for success with your taxes, whether paying as an individual or as a business, is to keep accurate and good books and records with as much detail and back up as you can in terms of forms, receipts, payments, and expenses. Also, don't spend more money than you make, and don't do it all yourself. Reach out to people who can help you, whether that's an attorney, an insurance agent, an accountant, a CPA, or a banker. People get in trouble when they're too proud to admit they need help.

If you are an employed individual, your tax process will likely be simple. You should receive the forms from your employer to fill out the W-4, for example, and the taxes are taken out of your paycheck every two weeks, or sometimes monthly. If you are self-employed, however, or run a business, it will take more thought and effort to make sure you're doing everything by the book. If you have a lot of employees, or don't know much about filing taxes, you will probably want to work with an expert. You'll want to take the time to hire the right accountant, someone who can work with you throughout the year to help you keep track of income and spending, and not just when it's time to prepare the tax return.

Working with a professional throughout the year will also help you see how you're doing in terms of growth or where you might need to make changes or tighten your belt a little. This is a good long-term strategy since most businesses are looking to last more than a few years. They want longevity. It may seem counterproductive to hire a tax professional and pay more money to save money, but I see it more as an investment to bring about greater long-term success.

Another best practice is to always make sure the income you report matches the 1099s you get from the IRS. Otherwise, you're sending a big red flag, and the IRS will come around sooner or later to see what's going on. I've stressed keeping good records throughout this book, but again, that's the key to staying out of trouble with the IRS. The more thorough and accurate you can be during the year, not just at tax season, the better you will be overall. If you can't afford a professional, you can invest in a basic version of accounting software. There are plenty online that are user-friendly for all the non-CPAs out there.

Another good business principle and practice is to make sure you have properly classified your business. If you don't do this, you could end up overpaying, which nobody wants, ever. You'll need to know if your company is a C corporation, S corporation, or LLC, for example, because they will have different effects on the taxes you pay. If you're not sure, you can ask an attorney to be safe.

It may seem obvious to keep your personal and business expenses separate, but you'd be surprised how many people accidentally don't do this or do it once or twice and think nobody will notice. If you mix the expenses too much, or inaccurately, the IRS might investigate your personal accounts, and the results could be fines for you. To keep it simple, you should get a separate bank account and credit card for the business, and run the business expenses through those only. Even if the mix-up happens only once, you may be putting your business in dangerous territory.

Another thing to know is that if you hire a company to help you with payroll, you don't want to skimp on that, especially if you have a business with a lot of employees. If you hire someone who doesn't have a lot of experience, is lazy, or doesn't understand when or how to pay payroll taxes, you'll be penalized because you are the owner of the company.

You can always go to the IRS website to see what is the latest in terms of rules and laws. If you don't have time or find that overwhelming, consult with your accountant. A good accountant can give you advice on how to grow the business and how to save money in the long term.

Use the Law to Your Advantage

New York State Justice Learned Hand once said, "There's nothing illegal in someone arranging their affairs to pay the least amount of tax as legally possible."[1] The operative word being *legally*. For example, if you have a business, you're allowed to have a retirement plan. You're allowed to contribute to that retirement plan, which is straightforward

---

1   Gregory v. Helvering 69 F.2d 809, 810 (2d Cir, 1934)

enough, but then some people don't realize that there are six different types of retirement plans that you can use. The question then becomes, which one is best for you? That will depend on what your business is, how big it is, and how much you're making.

Another example of using the law to your advantage is to know that you're allowed to write off the cost of equipment, furniture, and computers—anything really—that you buy for business purposes. To not do so would cost you money, but there are specific ways to write those things off. My office takes advantage of that every time new equipment is needed. But sometimes, it might not be beneficial for you to write everything off during the year, because next year you'll be in a higher tax bracket. Then what you want to do is shift deductions to lower your tax bracket next year, which just means paying less taxes overall.

It's better to work with a professional in these specific cases, of course, because you want to do everything by the book. There are people who spend their free time searching the internet for tax deductions and things like that. Sometimes they get it right, but sometimes they don't. When that happens, the cost isn't worth it, nor is the effort and time they spent. The law is there for your benefit. So while you may not be able to use all the benefits that somebody like Warren Buffet or Bill Gates might be using, you can still take advantage of the benefits appropriate for you and your situation.

I'll close this section with some additional ways of how you can pay fewer taxes or use tax law to your benefit. The first, which we went over briefly, is to apply for the EITC, which can help reduce the amount of tax you owe, based on the income you earn. You will need to meet certain requirements and file a tax return, and all this can be found online. The second credit is the Child Tax Credit (CTC), which will be based on your income and how many qualifying children you have. Under the CTC, children aged seventeen and younger are worth a certain dollar tax credit, based on your income. Tax credits reduce your tax liability dollar for dollar. This was expanded during COVID, so you'll want to check and see what the current benefits are.

Tax benefits can also help with education-related expenses, which includes tuition, student loans, books, and apprenticeship programs. You'll need to check and see if you qualify, and the institution has to be a qualifying one as well. This is something many don't do, and it applies to elementary schools, secondary schools, and colleges, as well as classes that help improve job skills. Given how expensive schooling is in this country, it's worth looking into. It can make a big difference to those who don't have a lot of, or any, disposable income.

You can also take advantage of energy-related tax incentives for home or business needs. Say, for example, you buy energy-efficient appliances, solar panels, solar water heaters, or biodiesel, then those may fall under residential energy credits. Depending on your state, you may also have benefits for other areas. In terms of natural disasters, you can get special tax help, outside an extension, and get faster returns. These forms are also available online and can help in especially hard times.

There are itemized deductions and standards that you can look to, either through the IRS website or with the help of a professional. Things such as property tax, sales tax, interest expense, and moving expenses may fall into these categories. You can also claim a deduction if you donated to a 501(c)(3) organization. For this, you will need to file a Schedule A with your tax return to then claim cash donations or a vehicle donation. If it is noncash, you may have to fill out a different form and will need to figure out the fair market value of the item. Limits exist here, of course, so you'll want to make sure you have records and proper documentation to back up the donations.

As with everything when it comes to the IRS, make sure you're playing by the rules. The IRS has strategies in place to make sure both individuals and business don't abuse their privileges. They will not take kindly to any falsifying or withholding of information. Hopefully after reading this section, you'll feel more confident about taking advantage of the law and are aware that you can make it work for you.

How I've Turned My Life Around

One of the reasons I was able to turn my life around and bounce back in my business is because I have a great deal of empathy. I've gone through a lot of what my clients are going through, and I'm transparent with them when I need to be. I'm not ashamed of my past, and in fact, it helps me connect more with people now. I owe the IRS money that I'm paying off now and am very close to being done with. I'm not judgmental with my clients or anyone who comes into my office to talk to me about their situation. I understand that life happens. After they explain where they are, I usually start with getting their taxes filed to set them on the right path and keep them clean going forward. I believe this is why a lot of people come to me and why they tell others about me.

The only exceptions I make when it comes to clients and cases is that I don't take criminal cases because I'm not an attorney. If a situation looks like it's turning criminal, I have attorneys that I work with, and they can hire me so that I can work under them and have attorney-client privilege. For example, if you came to me and said, "Hey, Jon, two people with badges came to my work yesterday and threatened to send me to jail because I owe taxes," I would tell you to see an attorney who could hire me to file your tax returns, among other things, but otherwise it's out of my jurisdiction. I'm not versed in criminal law; I can deal with numbers, taxes, and the IRS, but the rest is out of my hands.

Overall, though, I'd say that I'm flexible because I don't just work with doctors or dentists who have tax problems, or someone who is a few thousand dollars in debt. I'll look at what you have going on and let you know in a timely manner if I can help. What I don't do is lead people on or make them promises I can't keep. That's what a lot of these places that you see on late-night TV or on the radio do. They'll send you countless emails. I know because they still send them to me. Don't believe any emails or calls from people saying something like, "By reviewing your IRS case, I found out that I can reduce your debt by up to 70 percent. It is time-sensitive, so give me a call so that we can discuss your options." Such nonsense is too good to be true. How do they even know what your case is about?

Outside of being empathetic and nonjudgmental, I'm a hard worker who does everything I can to help you out of whatever situation you've gotten yourself into. A lot of people call me or show up in my office in tears, ready to give up because they can't see any clear path out of the money they owe, the payments they can't make, or the mess their documents are in. They might not have any documents at all, or they might be completely overwhelmed because they haven't paid their taxes in so long. Again, I understand all that. I've been there. There's no reason to be scared. I would encourage anyone out there who is, to do yourself a favor and reach out to me and get your life turned around. Admitting that you need help is the first step. From there, we'll create a viable plan for your financial success for now and into the future.

Acknowledgments

To my family: my wife and our children and my sister
and late brother-in-law

To my work family: Breann, Brittanie, Judy, and Kim

About the Author

The Neal Group LLC was founded in 1984 by Jon Neal, CPA, MST, CPFP, CTP. Jon has over forty years of experience in public accounting. In 1977, he graduated from the University of Wisconsin-Milwaukee with a BBA in Accounting and Management Information Systems, and in 1987, he earned his Master of Science in Taxation (MST).

In 1980, Jon received his Certified Public Accountant (CPA) license from the State of Wisconsin. He is especially focused on closely held businesses and their owners to help them reach their goals.

As a Certified Profit First Professional (CPFP), Jon works with businesses to keep more cash in their pockets. In addition to small business accounting, as a Certified Tax Master (CTM), Jon does extensive tax planning and tax resolution for individuals and businesses. Jon is a bestselling author, having written five books on various tax and accounting topics, and has appeared on several podcasts and television and radio shows.

Jon established Right Choice Tax Resolution Services, LLC, in 2018 to help businesses and individuals having issues with the IRS or State tax authorities. Jon and his team file delinquent returns, negotiate payment plans, negotiate offers in compromise, and serve as the lead person on tax audits to relieve stress so you can sleep at night.

Personally, Jon enjoys singing in his church's choir, spending time with his family, and volunteering. Jon and his wife, Ann, live in Hales Corners and have four children and six grandchildren.

For a free consultation, call 414-325-2040 or visit https://nealgroup.net or rightchoicetax.us.

Made in the USA
Columbia, SC
05 October 2022

68529706R00059